When POTENTIAL
Meets PURPOSE

A Journey of Discovery, Growth and Divine Assignment

By Melissa McDuffie and Kenneth McDuffie

WORKBOOK

WHEN POTENTIAL MEETS PURPOSE

COPYRGHT

WHEN POTENTIAL MEETS PURPOSE

DEDICATION

This work is tenderly and reverently dedicated to our mothers. Women who were living epistles, read by all, whose very breath carried the fragrance of Heaven.

They showed the world what it looks like when potential bows to purpose, when a life fully yielded becomes a vessel of divine legacy.

First, they served their families as if tending a sacred altar. Then, their neighbors, as if every handshake were a covenant and even strangers, as if they were entertaining angels unaware.

Their footsteps were psalms. Their hands, instruments of grace. Their words, quiet prophecies that shaped generations.

Every day, without pulpit or spotlight, they preached faith, modeled grace, and embodied strength that did not clamor for attention, but could not be ignored. Because of them, we stand. Because of them, we believe. Because of them, we are.

Queens, we crown you with our gratitude. Thank you for being the pattern, the prayer, and the proof. Thank you for living your testimony out loud, even in your silent tears.

Rest now, crowned with glory, in the unending embrace of His presence. Your assignment is complete, but your impact echoes in eternity.

WHEN POTENTIAL MEETS PURPOSE

FOREWORD

It has been both a joy and an honor to witness the spiritual growth of Melissa and Kenneth McDuffie. As their spiritual leaders, we've watched them walk faithfully through seasons of discovery, development, and divine assignment. Their obedience to God's voice and their passion for helping others fulfill their calling shine through every page of this book.

When Potential Meets Purpose is a timely reminder that our God-given potential isn't confined to the four walls of the Ecclesia. Melissa and Kenneth remind us that purpose goes far beyond the sanctuary, it's found in how we live, love, serve, and show up in our everyday lives.

This book encourages readers to be free from the opinions and comparisons of others, to walk boldly in their God-given identity, and to embrace the unique purpose God has placed within them. It also nudges those who already know their purpose but have grown complacent to develop and steward what God has placed in their hands.

Every chapter invites reflection and alignment, pushing us to see ourselves the way God sees us. Melissa and Kenneth have written a message that will awaken potential, stir purpose, and remind every reader that when potential meets purpose, destiny unfolds.

With Love and Kingdom Blessings,

Apostles D.C and Tara Terry

WHEN POTENTIAL MEETS PURPOSE

When Potential Meets Purpose is a short and simple to read, yet extremely powerful! This book will be a favorite because the message it brings is encouraging no matter what challenges a person is going through.

The first prayer says, "Help me to see myself the way You see me!" The rest of the book confirms that prayer. In addition, a declaration and prayer follow each lesson. Each prayer is on point and allows readers to pray when they are not sure what to pray for.

I would recommend this book to readers who are mature in Christ as a source of truth and encouragement as well as to young Christians who need to believe in what their desires are telling them.

Dr. Vickie Dexter

WHEN POTENTIAL MEETS PURPOSE

This book, When Potential Meets Purpose, is not merely a motivational guide or a collection of inspirational thoughts. It is a prophetic journey. A divine summons. A clarion call to become. With every chapter, you will feel the breath of God awakening what has long been dormant, overlooked, or buried beneath fear and delay. You will be reminded that the potential within you is not wishful thinking, it is Kingdom seed waiting for activation.

The authors write with the wisdom of one who has walked through the valley of obscurity and emerged carrying oil. Each word is saturated with both grace and truth, drawing from the wells of Scripture and the experiences of real lives transformed when God's plan breaks through human limitation. You will not only be inspired, you will be provoked to action.

We live in an hour where heaven is demanding a return on what it has invested. The cry of the Spirit is not just for church attendance but for Kingdom fulfillment. The earth groans for the manifestation of the sons and daughters of God (Romans 8:19). That manifestation begins when potential aligns with purpose. When the gift becomes governed. When the heart says, "Yes, Lord," even when the full path isn't clear.

If you have ever felt hidden, silenced, or unsure of your value; this book will be a healing balm. If you are standing at the crossroads of transition, unsure which way to go; this book will shine light on the path. And if you know you were born for more, but don't know how to access it, this book will give you language, direction, and courage.

You were created in the image of a creative God. That means there is innovation in your hands, solutions in your voice, and impact in your very being. But none of it is accidental. You were formed with intent. Designed with destiny. And now, you are being summoned into fulfillment.

As you turn these pages, do so prayerfully. Read with expectation. Highlight with boldness. And most of all, respond with surrender.

Because when potential meets purpose, heaven and earth collide and destiny is born.

With Love and expectation,

Apostle Pamela B Wise

WHEN POTENTIAL MEETS PURPOSE

INTRODUCTION & REFLECTION

Every journey begins with a divine spark; a moment when potential awakens, and purpose whispers its name.

In these pages, you are invited to recognize the image of God within you, to confront what silences your courage, and to embrace the process by which Heaven matures destiny. May each chapter be a doorway into alignment with the purpose for which you were sent.

WITH GRATITUDE

We offer our heartfelt thanks to every intercessor, mentor, friend, and family member who believed, prayed, and partnered with us. Your faith and love have been instruments in God's hands, shaping this journey from potential to purpose.

Melissa & Kenneth McDuffie

Contents

WHEN POTENTIAL MEETS PURPOSE

INTRODUCTION

WHEN POTENTIAL MEETS PURPOSE

There is a defining moment in your life when your potential collides with your purpose. Potential is the capacity God placed within you. Purpose is why He placed you here.

Have you ever felt like your potential was overlooked? Maybe you have been the dependable one, the background support, the quiet strength in the room, yet rarely seen for who you really are. You have carried dreams that others dismissed. You have gifts you were not quite sure how to use. And over time, perhaps you started to wonder, "Does any of this really matter?"

Let me reassure you, it matters deeply. Your potential is not some vague possibility; it is divine evidence that God planted something powerful inside of you. It does not require a platform or a perfect track record. What it needs is a yes. A willingness to believe that you were made for more, even if you cannot see the full picture yet.

You were born with kingdom potential, not by accident, but by divine design. Before you ever took your first breath, heaven had already written your blueprint for your life (Jeremiah 1:5). Your potential is not measured by what others can see, but by what God has already placed within you.

This book is for every person who knows there is more. More to become. More to give. More to activate. As you journey through each chapter, may you uncover hidden strength, heal from what held you back, and awaken the calling within you. Because when potential meets purpose, destiny is revealed.

There is a journal page after each chapter, please use it for your action steps and prompts, reflect on your answers as you grow.

WHEN POTENTIAL MEETS PURPOSE

Week 1 – Understanding Potential

There comes a moment when God whispers, "You already carry what you have been praying for." Understanding potential means realizing that Heaven has already invested something powerful inside you. You do not need another sign; you need to surrender. Each step of obedience draws out what has been lying dormant.

When you trust what God placed in you, your ordinary days become holy ground. Every decision becomes a seed, every act of faith a spark that awakens what has been waiting. Walking it out means letting God teach you how to move with confidence in what He already called complete.

Reflection: Today, ask yourself: Am I walking as if I truly believe that Heaven has invested potential within me? Let your next step reflect your faith in His design, not your doubt about your ability.

Weekly Prayer

Father, thank You for the potential You placed within me before I ever took my first breath. Help me to recognize the divine deposit that lives inside of me. Silence every voice of doubt that tells me I am not enough. Let me see myself through Your eyes, crafted, chosen, and capable. Show me that every gift and dream You have placed in me still carries power and purpose. Teach me to embrace the process that awakens what You planted. I surrender my fears, my limitations, and my need for perfection. Today, I say yes to growth, yes to purpose, and yes to becoming all You designed me to be. In Jesus Name Amen.

Scripture Meditation

Jeremiah 1:5

"Before I formed thee in the belly I knew thee; and before thou camest forth out of the womb I sanctified thee, and I ordained thee a prophet unto the nations."

WHEN POTENTIAL MEETS PURPOSE

Real-Life Reflection

Potential often hides in plain sight. A quiet woman once served faithfully as a church secretary, convinced her job was insignificant. But when her pastor became ill, she began coordinating volunteers, managing prayer lines, and encouraging others daily. Over time, her leadership blossomed, and she was appointed ministry director. The gifts she thought were "small" became the very tools God used to impact many. Her story reminds us: potential is not something you find, it is something you awaken.

Day 1 – What Is Potential

Devotional: Potential is the divine deposit of what could be the invisible promise of everything God placed inside of you. Before the world gave you a name, God gave you purpose. Potential is Heaven's investment in the earth through your life. It is not about talent or titles; it is about divine capacity waiting for movement. You do not have to earn potential; you already carry it. What God planted in you still has power, even if it feels buried.

Declaration: I was created with divine potential. What God placed in me will not die dormant, it will be developed and released for His glory.

Prayer: Lord, open my eyes to see the treasures You have placed within me. Silence every lie that says I am not enough. Let faith rise where fear once lived. Teach me to value the gifts You have entrusted to me. May I never bury what You designed to bless others.

Prompt: What ability, idea, or gift do you sense God has placed in you that you have overlooked?

Action Step: Write one area of potential you want to develop this week and take a small step toward it.

Day 2 – When Potential Shows Up

Devotional: Potential often appears in hidden places, before success, before applause, even before confidence. It shows up in wilderness season, in frustration, in the quiet space where no one is watching. Jeremiah's calling came before his experience. Likewise, your potential exists long before your platform. God is preparing you, even when you cannot see progress. The moment you surrender to His process is the moment potential begins to move.

Declaration: My potential is already in motion. Even in hidden seasons, God is preparing me for purpose.

Prayer: Father, thank You for working behind the scenes of my life. Help me to trust the process even when I do not see progress. Strengthen my patience and deepen my faith. Remind me that Your timing is perfect and that my development is sacred.

Prompt: Where in your life have you felt overlooked, but now realize God might be preparing you?

Action Step: Spend 10 minutes today thanking God for the hidden seasons that have shaped your strength.

Day 3 – Who Has Potential

Devotional: Everyone carries potential because everyone was created by God. Potential is not reserved for a select few, it is embedded in all who bear His image. The mother nurturing her children, the janitor praying over classrooms, the student journaling dreams, all are living examples of potential at work. Never compare your capacity to another is calling. If God gave you breath, He gave you purpose, and within that purpose lies power.

Declaration: I am fearfully and wonderfully made. God's potential in me is unique and unstoppable.

Prayer: Lord, thank You for making me in Your image. Forgive me for comparing my journey to others. Help me to embrace my uniqueness and use it to serve You boldly. Show me the value of what You have placed within me.

WHEN POTENTIAL MEETS PURPOSE

Prompt: What makes your gifts or story unique? How might God use that uniqueness to impact others?

Action Step: Encourage one person today by reminding them of the potential you see in them.

Day 4 – Where Potential Leads

Devotional: Potential does not lead to applause; it leads to alignment. It draws you into places that stretch your faith and refine your focus. Joseph's potential led him from a pit to a palace. David's led him from a pasture to the throne. Ruth's led her from loss to legacy. God's path may not always be easy, but it is always purposeful. Your potential will lead you through processes that shape your character before they reveal your calling.

Declaration: I trust where God is leading me. My potential will take me where purpose requires me to grow.

Prayer: Father, I surrender to Your leading. Even when the journey feels uncertain, help me to trust that You are guiding me. Align my steps with Your will. Refine my heart so I can carry Your purpose with grace.

Prompt: Where do you sense God leading you in this season of your life?

Action Step: Pray specifically over one area where you feel God is calling you to grow.

Day 5 – Activate the Assignment

Devotional: Potential without pursuit remains buried. Activation happens when obedience meets opportunity. Like Moses at the burning bush, your yes releases Heaven's power. You do not need to have everything figured out, you just need to move. God's power flows through motion. When you take one step, He multiplies it with grace. Do not wait for perfect timing; purpose begins when you do.

Declaration: I am moving from potential to purpose. My yes is the key that unlocks what God placed within me.

Prayer: Lord, thank You for trusting me with potential. Give me

WHEN POTENTIAL MEETS PURPOSE

boldness to move in obedience. Break the spirit of fear and hesitation. Let faith be my compass and surrender my strength. Use my yes to make impact for Your glory.

Prompt: What dream, goal, or idea have you delayed out of fear?

Action Step: Take one faith step this week toward something God has been nudging you to do.

Week 1 Kingdom Expansion: Understanding Potential

Teaching Spotlight: What the Bible Says

Genesis 1:26 declares, "Let us make man in our image, after our likeness…"
That means potential was your first inheritance. You were created with divine capacity, the same creative breath that spoke light into darkness now lives in you.

Jeremiah 1:5 echoes this truth: "Before I formed thee in the belly I knew thee."
Before you were named, you were known. Before you were seen, you were sent. You did not stumble into potential; you were sculpted with it.

Ephesians 3:20 affirms that God "is able to do exceeding abundantly above all that we ask or think, according to the power that worketh in us." That power is already at work; it only needs your agreement.

Your potential is not waiting for permission; it is waiting for participation. Heaven has already said yes.

Teaching Spotlight – Week 1: Understanding Potential

Potential is the seed of destiny God planted within you before time began. It is not discovered through striving but through surrender. From Genesis to Jeremiah, we see a God who calls out what He has already placed inside.

To understand potential is to realize that Heaven's design is already complete, you are simply walking out the unveiling. The same Spirit that hovered over the waters now hovers over your life, brooding over every buried dream, whispering, "Become."

When you yield to His voice, potential moves from concept to calling. It awakens in prayer, matures in obedience, and manifests through purpose. The enemy's goal is to convince you that you are empty; God's truth reminds you that you are overflowing.

You are not waiting for power; you are hosting it. Every yes refines the seed. Every act of faith pulls destiny closer. Understanding potential means seeing yourself as Heaven sees you: fully equipped, divinely resourced, and already chosen.

_____

_____

_____

_____

_____

_____

_____

_____

_____

_____

_____

_____

_____

_____

_____

_____

_____

_____

_____

_____

_____

_____

_____

_____

WHEN POTENTIAL MEETS PURPOSE

Week 2 – Understanding Purpose

Purpose does not begin when everything makes sense; it begins when you move in faith, even while it does not. Understanding purpose is not about chasing assignments, it is about aligning with the Author. Every chapter of your life, even the ones you would rather erase, holds revelation about why you are here.

God is not asking for your perfection, He is inviting your participation. When you walk in daily surrender, you start to see His fingerprints in what once felt random. Your life begins to flow with divine rhythm, and you realize that every "yes" you give Him is writing another line of your purpose story.

Reflection: Pause and thank God for the journey that brought you here. Write one area of your life where you now see His purpose working through what once felt painful or unclear.

Weekly Prayer

Father, thank You for designing my life with divine intention. I know that I am not here by accident, but by assignment. Open my heart to understand Your purpose in every season. When I feel uncertain, remind me that You never waste experiences, you weave them together for good. Help me to walk in clarity, not confusion; in faith, not fear. Reveal the reason behind my process and let every step I take draw me closer to what You originally had in mind for me. Align my thoughts with Heaven's plan and let purpose rise within me until it overflows. In Jesus' Name, Amen.

Scripture Meditation

Romans 8:28

"And we know that all things work together for good to them that love God, to them who are the called according to his purpose."

Real-Life Reflection

Purpose is rarely discovered all at once. A young woman once

dreamed of being a teacher, but life detoured her through caregiving for an elderly relative. What she thought delayed her destiny actually developed her compassion, patience, and leadership. Years later, when she became a teacher, those same qualities transformed her classroom into a place of healing and hope. Purpose is not a position; it is progression. Every detour is part of the divine design.

Day 1 – What Is Purpose

Devotional: Purpose is the reason something exists. It is Heaven's "why" behind your "what." Purpose answers the question: Why am I here? You were created with a divine assignment that connects your gifts to God's greater plan. Purpose is not something you invent, it is something you uncover through intimacy with the Creator. When you understand purpose, you no longer chase approval; you follow alignment.

Declaration: I was created on purpose, for purpose, with purpose.

Prayer: Lord, show me the "why" behind my existence. Help me to see beyond daily tasks and recognize Your eternal plan in my life. Strip away distractions and help me focus on what truly matters, fulfilling Your will.

Prompt: What does purpose mean to you right now, and how has your understanding of it changed over time?

Action Step: Write a one-sentence statement describing what you believe your God-given purpose involves today.

Day 2 – When Purpose Is Revealed

Devotional: Purpose is revealed in God's timing, not yours. Moses did not step into purpose until he turned aside to see the burning bush. David's anointing came years before his crown. Jesus waited thirty years before releasing three years of ministry. Delay does not mean denial, it means development. God reveals purpose when your character can carry it.

Declaration: I trust God's timing for my purpose. What He started, He will finish in His perfect season.

Prayer: Father, forgive me for rushing ahead of Your timing. Teach me to trust the process that leads to purpose. Strengthen me in the waiting and help me discern what You are building in me before You release me into it.

Prompt: What season are you currently in, preparation, positioning, or purpose in action?

Action Step: Identify one area where God is teaching you patience and thank Him for what He is developing in you there.

Day 3 – Who Has Purpose

Devotional: Every life carries divine purpose. The same God who set the stars in place also set your destiny. You do not need a platform to have purpose; your obedience is your platform. God uses ordinary people to fulfill extraordinary plans. The fisherman became an apostle, the shepherd became a king, the orphan became a deliverer. Your background does not disqualify you; it often reveals where God's glory will shine brightest.

Declaration: I am chosen and called for purpose. My past cannot cancel my calling.

Prayer: Lord, thank You for choosing me before I chose You. Help me to stop disqualifying myself. Show me that You have assigned meaning to every moment of my life. Use me right where I am and let my obedience reveal Your glory.

Prompt: What labels or limitations have you believed that might be

keeping you from walking fully in your purpose?

Action Step: Write down a truth from Scripture that replaces one of those false limitations.

Day 4 – Where Purpose Leads

Devotional: Purpose will always lead you to people and places that stretch you. It leads you beyond comfort zones and into Kingdom assignments. When God calls you to something greater, it will often require you to let go of what feels familiar. Purpose leads you to promise, but not without process. Every "yes" to God leads you deeper into destiny.

Declaration: My purpose will take me where my comfort cannot. I will follow God's direction with faith and courage.

Prayer: Father, lead me where my purpose calls me to go. Even when I do not see the full picture, I trust Your plan. Give me courage to obey even when the next step feels uncomfortable. Let Your will become my desire.

Prompt: Where do you sense God leading you to step out in faith right now?

Action Step: Take one small action this week that stretches your faith toward God's purpose for your life.

Day 5 – Walking in Purpose

Devotional: Purpose is not a destination; it is a daily decision. You walk in purpose when you align your thoughts, words, and actions with God's truth. Every "yes" to obedience moves you forward. Purpose is lived out in how you love, serve, forgive, and lead. It is not what you do once; it is who you choose to be every day.

Declaration: I walk in purpose daily. Every step I take is guided by God's plan for my life.

Prayer: Lord, help me to live purposefully. Let my schedule, my speech, and my service reflect Your will. Keep me sensitive to divine opportunities to represent You well. May my life be a walking testimony of Your purpose fulfilled.

Prompt: How can you walk intentionally in purpose today, in your home, work, or ministry?

Action Step: Choose one way to serve others today that aligns with your purpose and brings God glory.

Week 2 Kingdom Expansion: Understanding Purpose

Teaching Spotlight: What the Bible Says

Proverbs 19:21 declares, "Many are the plans in a person's heart, but it is the Lord's purpose that prevails." Purpose is not fragile, it is fixed.

Romans 8:28 assures us that "all things work together for good to them that love God." Even the detours of your life are direction in disguise.

Psalm 37:23 promises, "The steps of a good man are ordered by the Lord." Every step, forward, backward, or paused, is choreography in God's grand design.

> *Purpose is not a mystery you chase; it is a map you uncover through daily obedience.*

Teaching Spotlight – Week 2: Understanding Purpose

Purpose is the divine storyline hidden inside your journey. It is the "why" beneath your "what." You were not placed on earth to drift; you were deployed with intent.

From Abraham's obedience to Esther's courage, Scripture shows that purpose always emerges through process. God does not reveal the entire blueprint; He reveals the next step. Each act of obedience becomes a verse in your destiny's song.

Understanding purpose is realizing that you are both participant and product of Heaven's strategy. Your pain becomes prophetic training, your victories become testimonies, and your ordinary days become altars.

You are not searching for purpose; you are stewarding it. Every encounter, every assignment, every breath is wrapped in Kingdom significance. When potential is the what God gave you, purpose is the why He gave it. And when the two align, impact becomes inevitable.

WHEN POTENTIAL MEETS PURPOSE

_____

_____

_____

_____

_____

_____

_____

_____

_____

_____

_____

_____

_____

_____

_____

_____

_____

_____

_____

_____

_____

_____

_____

_____

_____

WHEN POTENTIAL MEETS PURPOSE

Week 3 – The Power of Potential

Maybe no one sees what you carry. Maybe your gifts have been overlooked, underestimated, or even dismissed, by others or by yourself. But Heaven sees. Heaven knows. And Heaven is waiting for your yes.

Potential is not about applause; it is about obedience. It whispers in the small steps: when you say yes to the next right thing, when you give even though it stretches you, when you forgive even when it hurts. That is what it means to walk in purpose, not by spotlight, but by surrender.

Some of the most powerful purpose stories began in obscure places. David was anointed but still had to go back to feeding sheep. Ruth found her destiny while picking up leftovers. Jesus, the Savior of the world, lived thirty quiet years before stepping into public ministry. Do not let quiet seasons make you question your calling. God does His best work in the dark soil before anything sprouts.

So today, do not ask God for visibility. Ask Him for vision. Ask Him to show you what you have been carrying all along. The dreams, the creativity, the insight, the faith, they are not random. They are Heaven's fingerprints on your soul.

And remember you do not have to be loud to be powerful. You just have to be faithful.

Weekly Prayer

Father, thank You for placing power within me through Your Spirit. Remind me that potential is not just possibility, it is power waiting to be activated. When I feel weak, teach me to rely on the strength that already lives in me. Stir up every gift that has been lying dormant. Let my words, my faith, and my obedience release Your power through my life. Make me bold to act, wise to discern, and faithful to finish. In Jesus' Name, Amen.

WHEN POTENTIAL MEETS PURPOSE

Ephesians 3:20

"Now unto him that is able to do exceedingly abundantly above all that we ask or think, according to the power that worketh in us."

Real-Life Reflection

A young man once volunteered to help with the church's media team, unsure of his ability. As he served, his skill and creativity began to flourish. Soon he was leading entire productions that reached thousands online. What started as hesitation became empowerment, proof that when you step out, God multiplies what is already inside you. Potential carries power, but it is released through participation.

Day 1 – Power Revealed

Devotional: The same power that raised Jesus from the dead dwells in you. This means potential is not passive, its divine power disguised as possibility. The moment you believe what God has placed in you, that power begins to work through you. Heaven's greatness lives within earthen vessels.

Declaration: The power of God is alive in me.

Prayer: Lord, help me to see myself as a vessel of Your power. Reveal what You have deposited within me and teach me to use it for Your glory.

Prompt: What does it mean to you that God's power is "working in you"?

Action Step: Write one way you can use your God-given strength to serve someone else this week.

WHEN POTENTIAL MEETS PURPOSE

Day 2 – Power Tested

Devotional: Power is proved through pressure. Every trial becomes a testing ground for what you carry. When resistance comes, it reveals your spiritual muscle. Just as oil comes from pressed olives, the anointing flows when potential is pressed.

Declaration: Pressure cannot break me; it builds me.

Prayer: Father, when I face opposition, remind me that You are developing my strength. Help me endure with grace and trust Your plan through the process.

Prompt: How has a recent challenge revealed your growth or faith?

Action Step: List one lesson your latest difficulty has taught you about your own strength in Christ.

Day 3 – Power Released

Devotional: Power is released through obedience. When you say yes to God, you become a conduit for miracles. The woman with the issue of blood touched Jesus in faith and power flowed out of Him. Your faith-filled actions draw Heaven into the earth. Potential is activated when you move in belief.

Declaration: My obedience unlocks God's power in my life.

Prayer: Lord, teach me to respond quickly when You speak. Let my faith be seen in my actions so Your power can flow freely through me.

Prompt: What step of obedience is God asking you to take now?

Action Step: Take that step today, no matter how small it seems

Day 4 – Power Multiplied

Devotional: When you steward power well, God multiplies it. Faithfulness with little invites increase. Every time you use your gift, you expand your capacity. Like the loaves and fishes, what you offer to God multiplies in His hands.

Declaration: As I use what God has given me, He multiplies it for impact.

WHEN POTENTIAL MEETS PURPOSE

Prayer: Father, make me a faithful steward of Your power. Increase my capacity to carry more of Your glory through humility and service.

Prompt: Where have you seen God multiply your efforts or gifts after you used them in faith?

Action Step: Find one area where you can stretch beyond your comfort zone and serve with excellence this week.

Day 5 – Power for Purpose

Devotional: The power of potential is never for personal gain; it is for Kingdom purpose. Power without purpose leads to pride, but power aligned with purpose leads to impact. God's power in you exists to heal, help, and bring hope to others. When you use your power for His plan, you fulfill your divine assignment.

Declaration: God's power in me is for God's purpose through me.

Prayer: Lord, use my life to demonstrate Your power and love. Keep my heart pure and my motives aligned with Your Kingdom. Let everything I do bring You glory.

Prompt: How can you use your abilities to serve a greater Kingdom cause this month?

Action Step: Commit to one specific way you will apply your power toward Kingdom impact.

Week 3 Kingdom Expansion: The Power of Potential

All throughout Scripture, we see a pattern: God calls out what He already placed within.

Jeremiah was told, "Before I formed you in the womb, I knew you…" **Jeremiah 1:5**. That means your potential predates your problems. Before your name was known on Earth, your destiny was established in Heaven.

Ephesians 2:10 says, "We are God's workmanship, created in Christ Jesus to do good works, which God prepared in advance for us to do." You were not made on accident, you were made on purpose, with purpose, for purpose.

And in **Matthew 25**, the Parable of the Talents reminds us that God does not just bless us with gifts, He expects us to multiply them. The Master praised the servants who invested and grew what they were given. But the one who buried his talent out of fear? He received rebuke, not reward.

God honors those who risk growth. He celebrates those who work their gifts, even when it is hard. He partners with those who move in faith, even if they feel small.

All throughout Scripture, we see a divine pattern unfold: God never asks us to become something He has not already placed within us. His call is not a reaction to our capacity; it is a revelation of what He already deposited.

When God spoke to Jeremiah, He did not begin with an assignment. He began with identity: "Before I formed you in the womb, I knew you…" (Jeremiah 1:5). That is not poetic language, it is prophetic truth. Your potential predates your problems. Your purpose existed long before your pain. Heaven had plans for you before you ever had a name on Earth.

Ephesians 2:10 takes it deeper: "We are God's workmanship, created in Christ Jesus to do good works, which God prepared in advance for us to do." You were not mass-produced. You were handcrafted. Formed in Christ. Shaped by purpose. God did not improvise your destiny; He predesigned it with intentionality and love.

And in **Matthew 25,** Jesus shares the Parable of the Talents, not to entertain, but to awaken. The Master did not reward gifting alone, He rewarded growth. Those who risked faith, invested their talents, and multiplied what was given were praised and promoted. But the one who buried his potential out of fear was rebuked, not because he lacked ability, but because he lacked alignment.

Let this truth settle in your spirit: God honors motion. He partners with those who dare to move forward, even while feeling small. He rejoices over those who build in secret and steward what seems insignificant. Potential is not passive, it is prophetic. And the moment you believe that what He placed in you is enough, you become unstoppable in His hands.

_____

_____

_____

_____

_____

_____

_____

_____

_____

_____

_____

_____

_____

_____

_____

_____

_____

_____

_____

_____

_____

_____

_____

_____

WHEN POTENTIAL MEETS PURPOSE

Week 4 – Personal Potential

Maybe you have been taught that humility means hiding. That to be holy means to shrink. But true humility is not thinking less of yourself, it is thinking of yourself rightly through God's lens.

So, let me ask you: What if that quiet strength you carry is not random? What if your love for organizing, writing, mentoring, planning, teaching, what if those passions are not personality quirks, but divine blueprints?

So many of us wait for someone to call out what we know deep down is already there. But here is the truth: Heaven is not silent about your worth. God has already affirmed you. The question is, will you agree with Him?

If your soul feels unsettled, if your gifts feel underused, if your voice has been silenced by fear or fatigue, this is your wake-up call. You are not too late. You are not too much. You are not behind.

God is not looking for a polished version of you; He is looking for the surrendered version. He can work with honesty. He can shape humility. But He cannot multiply what you refuse to acknowledge.

Take inventory today. What do you love? What brings you joy? What do people naturally seek you out for? Hidden in those answers is a map to your personal potential.

Your authenticity is your anointing. And the world does not need another imitation, it needs you, fully awake and fully aligned with why you were made.

Weekly Prayer

Father, thank You for creating me in Your image and likeness. Help me to see myself through Your eyes, not through the lens of fear, failure, or comparison. Silence every voice that tells me I am not enough. Heal the places in me that have been bruised by rejection or doubt. Let Your truth restore my confidence and anchor my worth in who You are. Reveal the beauty, strength, and creativity You have placed

within me, and help me walk boldly in it. I am not a mistake; I am a masterpiece. In Jesus Name Amen.

Scripture Meditation

Genesis 1:26

"And God said, Let us make man in our image, after our likeness: and let them have dominion over the fish of the sea, and over the fowl of the air, and over the cattle, and over all the earth, and over every creeping thing that creepeth upon the earth."

Real-Life Reflection

Personal potential begins with personal identity. A young woman once struggled to believe in her worth after years of rejection. But when she discovered the truth of Genesis 1:26, that she was made in God's image, her mindset changed. She began speaking life over herself, journaling her dreams, and taking small steps of faith. Today she leads others into healing and confidence. Her story proves that when you know who you are, you begin to unlock what you carry.

Day 1 – Knowing Your Worth

Devotional: You were created intentionally. Every detail about you, your voice, your gifts, your passions, reflects the image of God. When you undervalue yourself, you insult your Creator's design. Personal potential begins when you believe you are valuable to God and capable through Him.

Declaration: I am fearfully and wonderfully made in the image of God.

Prayer: Lord, help me to see myself as You see me. Heal my heart from self-doubt and teach me to value who I am in You.

Prompt: What lies have shaped the way you see yourself, and what truth from God's Word can replace them?

Action Step: Write three affirmations rooted in Scripture that speak to your worth in God.

Day 2 – The Mirror of the Word

Devotional: The Word of God is the true mirror of your identity. When you look into Scripture, you see who you were always meant to be. The enemy distorts; the Word restores. As you meditate on truth, you begin to reflect His image more clearly. Transformation happens not by striving, but by seeing yourself through His Word.

Declaration: I reflect the image of God and walk in His truth.

Prayer: Father, let Your Word reveal who I truly am. Remove every false label and renew my mind with Your truth.

Prompt: What verse from Scripture best reminds you of who you are in Christ?

Action Step: Place that verse somewhere you will see it daily and speak it aloud each morning.

Day 3 – Breaking the Box

Devotional: People may try to define you by your past, but only God has the right to name you. Breaking the box means refusing to live within the limitations of others' opinions. True potential is unlocked when you stop fitting in and start standing out. You were never designed to blend in; you were designed to reflect glory.

Declaration: I am not confined by others' opinions; I am defined by God's truth.

Prayer: Lord, free me from every label, fear, or expectation that keeps me small. Let me walk boldly in my divine identity.

Prompt: What "boxes" have you allowed others to place you in, and how can you break free?

Action Step: Do one thing this week that expresses your authentic self, even if it feels uncomfortable

WHEN POTENTIAL MEETS PURPOSE

Day 4 – Chosen and Called

Devotional: You were not just created; you were chosen. God handpicked you for a purpose only you can fulfill. You may feel overlooked by people, but you are never overlooked by God. Calling begins with confidence in the One who called you. Your uniqueness is not a weakness; it is your Kingdom assignment.

Declaration: I am chosen and called for divine purpose.

Prayer: Father, thank You for choosing me. Help me to embrace the call You have placed on my life. Remove fear and fill me with courage to walk it out.

Prompt: What evidence can you see in your life that God has called you for something specific?

Action Step: Write down one area where you sense God's call and take one intentional step toward it this week.

Day 5 – Embracing Your Story

Devotional: Your story is not your shame; it is your strength. Every chapter, even the painful ones, carries a testimony of God's grace. Embracing your story means owning where you have been, acknowledging what God has redeemed, and allowing Him to use it for His glory. You are living proof that God can turn pain into purpose.

Declaration: My story matters because God is still writing it.

Prayer: Lord, thank You for redeeming my story. Use my journey to encourage others and bring hope where there was once hurt.

Prompt: What part of your story could bring healing or encouragement to someone else?

Action Step: Share one piece of your story with someone who needs hope this week.

WHEN POTENTIAL MEETS PURPOSE

Week 4 Kingdom Expansion: Personal Potential
Teaching Spotlight: What the Bible Says

Scripture gives us many glimpses into how personal identity and divine calling are connected:

Jeremiah 1:5, "Before I formed you in the womb, I knew you..."
God is intimately acquainted with your story, not just the parts you share, but the parts you have buried. Your identity is not formed by pain; it is formed by His purpose.

2 Peter 1:3, "His divine power has given us everything we need for life and godliness..."
You do not have to search endlessly for worth. It is already in you. You were equipped from day one to fulfill your assignment.

Romans 12:6, "We have different gifts, according to the grace given to each of us..."
Personal potential looks different for everyone. Embrace your difference. It is not a defect; it is your distinction.

You cannot maximize what you constantly minimize. Speak life over yourself. Honor how God wired you. Stop asking for permission to be what Heaven has already called you to be.

Teaching Spotlight – Week 4: Personal Potential

Your potential is not just about what you can do, it is about who you are becoming. Before God calls you to perform, He calls you to align. Potential is not developed by striving; it is awakened by identity.

Too often, we define ourselves by external roles or past failures, but God calls us by purpose, not performance. 2 Timothy 1:7 reminds us that "God hath not given us the spirit of fear; but of power, and of love, and of a sound mind." These are not just traits; they are your inheritance. When you fully embrace who you are in Christ, the grip of fear begins to break, and the truth of your design starts to emerge.

You were not created to live in comparison or apology. You were made to reflect a unique facet of the Father's glory. **Psalm 139** declares that you were fearfully and wonderfully made, not just formed, but authored. Every detail of your wiring, every nuance of your personality, every passion that burns quietly in your spirit is part of Heaven's blueprint for you.

But potential cannot be released in environments of doubt. It must be cultivated in atmospheres of truth, intimacy, and surrender. God reveals identity in quiet places so it cannot be shaken by noisy seasons. As you walk with Him, He begins to unearth the dormant seeds in your soul, the gifts you dismissed, the dreams you shelved, the assignments you thought were too big.

Personal potential is not a mystery; it is a mirror. When you look at Christ, you begin to see yourself rightly. The closer you move toward Him, the clearer your identity becomes. And from that place of clarity, courage is born. Courage to step out. Courage to speak up. Courage to pursue purpose with holy confidence.

You are not too late, too broken, or too ordinary. You are positioned

by Heaven and equipped with everything you need to become who God already saw. Personal potential is not something you earn, it is something you remember.

_____

_____

_____

_____

_____

_____

_____

_____

_____

_____

_____

_____

_____

_____

_____

_____

_____

_____

_____

_____

_____

_____

_____

WHEN POTENTIAL MEETS PURPOSE

Week 5 – Professional Potential

Maybe your current job feels far from your calling. Maybe your gifts feel stifled, your dreams shelved, your days repetitive. But let me assure you: God wastes nothing. Even this season, especially this season, holds purpose.

What if this job is not the destination, but the development?

What if the difficult coworker is refining your patience? What if the lack of recognition is anchoring your identity in Christ? What if this quiet season is building the character that your future platform will require?

Do not despise the training ground. Do not overlook the lesson hidden in the labor. God is preparing you for places you have not seen yet. But preparation only works when you are faithful in the now.

Purpose does not wait for promotion. It shows up in excellence right where you are.

So today, shift your perspective. Invite God into your workday. Ask Him to make your workplace a sanctuary. And then, show up differently. Answer emails with grace. Lead meetings with integrity. Speak life in the break room. Let your faith be visible not just in your words, but in your work ethic.

Your professionalism is part of your purpose.

Weekly Prayer

Father, thank You for the work You have placed in my hands. Help me to see my career, business, or daily tasks as holy opportunities to serve You. Let integrity guide my decisions and excellence define my efforts. Teach me to lead with grace, to serve with humility, and to honor You in everything I do. May my workplace become an altar of worship, and my diligence a reflection of Your glory. Use me as Your ambassador in the marketplace to bring light, wisdom, and transformation. In Jesus Name Amen.

Colossians 3:23

"And whatsoever ye do, do it heartily, as to the Lord, and not unto men."

Real-Life Reflection

A woman once felt frustrated in her job, convinced it was beneath her potential. But as she began to approach each task as if it were for God, her attitude changed, and so did her outcomes. Her diligence began attracting favor, and before long, she was promoted to a leadership role. The same office that felt like a cage became her platform. Purpose is not limited to the pulpit; it is revealed in every space where you choose to serve with excellence.

Day 1 – Work as Worship

Devotional: Your job is not just employment; it is an environment for Kingdom expression. God values your work because it reflects His creativity and order. When you give your best effort with the right heart, your labor becomes worship. Every meeting, task, and conversation can glorify God when done with integrity and joy.

Declaration: My work is an act of worship to God.

Prayer: Lord, help me to see my daily work as sacred service. Let my effort honor You and bless those around me.

Prompt: How might your attitude toward work change if you viewed it as worship?

Action Step: Begin your workday tomorrow with prayer, dedicating your labor to God.

Day 2 – The Anointed Professional

Devotional: The same Spirit that empowers preachers empowers professionals. God anointed craftsmen like Bezalel in Exodus 31 to build His tabernacle with skill and excellence. Your workplace is a mission field, and your anointing is your advantage. When you rely on the Holy Spirit, He gives you insight, creativity, and solutions that exceed human wisdom.

Declaration: I am anointed to lead, create, and excel in my work.

Prayer: Father, anoint my hands and mind to perform with excellence. Let Your Spirit inspire my creativity and guide my decisions.

Prompt: In what area of your work do you sense God wants to release new creativity or wisdom?

Action Step: Ask the Holy Spirit for fresh strategy for one task or project this week.

Day 3 – Integrity at Work

Devotional: Integrity is the foundation of Kingdom leadership. God honors those who are faithful even when no one is watching. When you do the right thing in secret, God rewards you in public. Integrity is not about perfection; it is about consistency in character. The world needs professionals whose values reflect Heaven's culture.

Declaration: I walk in integrity, even when it costs me comfort.

Prayer: Lord, help me to value honesty over image and character over convenience. Let my reputation reflect Your righteousness.

Prompt: Where are you being challenged to maintain integrity right now?

Action Step: Make one choice this week that prioritizes integrity over convenience.

WHEN POTENTIAL MEETS PURPOSE

Day 4 – Excellence Over Performance

Devotional: Performance seeks applause, but excellence seeks purpose. Excellence is not about doing more; it is about doing what matters most with the right heart. When you focus on excellence, you work from peace instead of pressure. God rewards diligence done in faith, not perfection done in fear.

Declaration: I choose excellence over performance.

Prayer: Father, free me from striving for human approval. Teach me to serve with grace, confidence, and excellence that glorifies You.

Prompt: What area of your work has become driven by performance rather than purpose?

Action Step: Identify one task or responsibility you can approach with fresh excellence instead of pressure.

Day 5 – Ministry in the Marketplace

Devotional: You are a minister disguised as a professional. Every conversation, meeting, or project can become an opportunity to display God's love and wisdom. The Kingdom advances when believers bring light into dark places. Your work matters to Heaven because it reveals God's heart to the world.

Declaration: I am a Kingdom representative in my workplace.

Prayer: Lord, help me to see my coworkers, clients, and supervisors as divine assignments. Let my words bring life and my actions reflect Your character.

Prompt: Who in your workplace or professional circle could benefit from encouragement or prayer?

Action Step: This week, intentionally show kindness or offer prayer to one person in your workplace.

Week 5 Kingdom Expansion: Professional Potential

Teaching Spotlight: What the Bible Says

Colossians 3:23 says, "Whatever you do, work at it with all your heart, as working for the Lord, not for human masters."

God does not categorize jobs by spiritual rank. He sees the janitor and the pastor the same when both are faithful. He measures obedience, not platform.

Consider Joseph. Before he ever governed Egypt, he served faithfully in Potiphar's house and in prison. His promotion came not from ambition, but from consistency. He did not wait for the palace to be excellent; he practiced excellence in the shadows.

Proverbs 22:29 declares, "Do you see a man skilled in his work? He will stand before kings…" Excellence is Kingdom language. It opens doors. It turns mundane moments into ministry moments.

So, whether you are behind a desk or behind a cash register, remember you are not just working, you are witnessing. You are not just paid, you are positioned.

Teaching Spotlight – Week 5: Professional Potential

God does not separate the sacred from the secular, He invades both. Your profession is not beneath His purpose. In fact, your workplace may be one of the greatest stages for Kingdom impact. It is not about preaching with a microphone, it is about building with integrity, leading with compassion, and showing up every day as someone Heaven can trust.

Colossians 3:23 reminds us, "And whatsoever ye do, do it heartily, as to the Lord, and not unto men." This verse reframes every task, big or small, as worship. Whether you are designing, managing, teaching, repairing, or serving, your work is spiritual when it is surrendered. When you labor with the awareness that God is your true supervisor, excellence becomes your standard, and honor becomes your language.

Too often, believers underestimate the influence hidden in their 9-to-5. But Joseph's favor was not first recognized on a throne, it was seen

in Potiphar's house and later in a prison. Daniel's prophetic insight was not limited to a temple; it operated in the government of Babylon. These men did not just carry anointing, they carried assignment. And that assignment prospered in professional environments.

Your gifts were never meant to be boxed into Sunday morning. They are designed to disrupt boardrooms, innovate solutions, heal broken systems, and carry the fragrance of the Kingdom into spaces where compromise has become the norm. God is looking for Daniels in data centers, Esthers in education, Nehemiah in nonprofit work, and Josephs in government.

Professional potential does not mean abandoning your career for full-time ministry. It means seeing your career as ministry. It means discerning the divine behind the demands of the day. It means asking not just "What do I do?" but "Who can I reach? What can I shift? How can I reflect Christ here?"

There is oil on your occupation. Heaven is not just watching your worship, it is watching your work ethic, your stewardship, your excellence. Your consistency on the job may be the very thing that softens a heart, opens a door, or prepares a nation. Do not discount your desk, it could be your altar.

_____

_____

_____

_____

_____

_____

_____

_____

_____

_____

_____

_____

_____

_____

_____

_____

_____

_____

_____

_____

_____

_____

_____

WHEN POTENTIAL MEETS PURPOSE

Week 6 – Developmental Potential

Maybe you are in a season that feels stagnant. You are praying but not hearing much. You are showing up but not seeing fruit. You are trying to grow, but you feel more like you are surviving.

Let me encourage you: you are not stuck; you are being stretched. And stretching seasons are holy ground.

God does His best work in the hidden places, the late nights where no one sees your tears, the quiet sacrifices you make that no one acknowledges, the battles you fight in your mind that no one knows about. These are not wasted moments. They are the gym where spiritual muscles are formed.

Think about trees. Before they ever grow tall, they grow deep. Their root systems expand underground to prepare them for what is coming above. Likewise, the strength God is building in you today is preparing you to stand strong tomorrow.

You may still struggle with old patterns. You may have moments of relapse or doubt. But do not disqualify yourself because you have not "arrived." None of us have. Growth is not about perfection; it is about direction. Are you still showing up? Still seeking God? Still taking small steps? Then you are growing.

Do not rush the process. Do not resent the pruning. Lean into the season you are in and ask God, "What are You developing in me right now?"

Because every stretch, every surrender, every hidden yes is producing a harvest that will last.

Weekly Prayer

Father, thank You for being patient with me as You develop what You have placed within me. Remind me that every season, whether stretching, pruning, or pressing, is working for my growth. When I do not understand the process, help me trust the Potter's hand. Shape me, refine me, and complete every good work You have begun in me. Teach me to see progress even when I cannot see perfection.

WHEN POTENTIAL MEETS PURPOSE

May I yield to Your timing and walk faithfully through each stage of development. In Jesus Name, Amen.

Scripture Meditation

Philippians 1:6

"Being confident of this very thing, that he which hath begun a good work in you will perform it until the day of Jesus Christ."

Isaiah 64:8

"But now, O Lord, thou art our father; we are the clay, and thou our potter; and we all are the work of thy hand."

Real-Life Reflection

A young entrepreneur once prayed for success but instead faced constant setbacks. Every door that closed seemed like failure until she realized God was developing her character, not delaying her destiny. The very experiences she called "hard seasons" became her greatest training ground. When she finally stepped into her calling, she had both strength and humility. Development is God's design for durability; He shapes us in private so we can withstand in public.

Day 1 – Growing Through Process

Devotional: Growth requires process. Every seed must go through hidden seasons before it bears fruit. God is not just preparing blessings for you; He is preparing you for them. The process is not punishment, it is preparation.

Declaration: I embrace the process that prepares me for purpose.

Prayer: Lord, help me not to resist the seasons that develop me. Let me grow through what I go through.

Prompt: What area of your life is currently in development, and what lesson might God be teaching you through it?

Action Step: Write one area where you need to trust God's timing instead of rushing the outcome.

Day 2 – The Power of Patience

Devotional: Patience is not passive; it is powerful. Waiting on God strengthens your faith and builds endurance. While you wait, God works. Patience teaches you to rest in His promises rather than strive in your own strength.

Declaration: I will wait well because God is working while I wait.

Prayer: Father, teach me to wait with faith, not frustration. Help me to see the beauty in becoming.

Prompt: How do you usually respond when God's timing does not match your expectation?

Action Step: Practice patience today by pausing before you respond to a challenging situation or decision.

Day 3 – Lessons in the Wilderness

Devotional: The wilderness is a classroom, not a curse. God used the wilderness to train Israel for the Promised Land. What feels like isolation is often preparation. It is where distractions fade and dependence on God deepens. Do not despise the dry places, they are developing your discernment.

Declaration: My wilderness is working for my wisdom.

Prayer: Lord, help me to learn the lessons hidden in lonely seasons. Teach me to trust You when I cannot trace You.

Prompt: What season in your life once felt like a wilderness but later revealed divine lessons?

Action Step: Journal one key lesson from your current or past wilderness season and how it has strengthened your faith.

Day 4 – Refined for Purpose

Devotional: Refinement comes through fire, but it produces glory. Like gold in the furnace, you are purified through testing. God allows refinement not to destroy you, but to define you. The heat removes impurities so His image can shine through.

Declaration: I am refined, not ruined by the fire.

Prayer: Father, help me to endure refinement with grace. Burn away what does not belong so I can reflect Your glory.

Prompt: What has God refined in your character through recent challenges?

Action Step: Thank God for one area of your life that has been purified through hardship

Day 5 – Maturity in Motion

Devotional: Maturity is not measured by knowledge but by consistency. Development continues as you live out what you have learned. Spiritual maturity means choosing obedience over emotion and wisdom over impulse. God develops you daily through discipline.

Declaration: I am growing stronger, wiser, and more consistent every day.

Prayer: Lord, mature me through obedience. Help me to apply what You have taught me and to walk worthy of my calling.

Prompt: What does maturity look like for you in this season?

Action Step: Choose one daily habit that will strengthen your spiritual growth and commit to it this week.

Week 6 Kingdom Expansion: Developmental Potential

Teaching Spotlight: What the Bible Says

In **Hebrews 12:11**, we are told: "No discipline seems pleasant at the time, but painful. Later on, however, it produces a harvest of

righteousness and peace..." This verse does not glamorize the pruning process. It tells the truth, growth often hurts. But it also promises fruit.

Every time you say yes to God's refining work, He is shaping you into someone who can carry more. More responsibility. More influence. More depth.

Another key verse is **2 Timothy 1:7:** "For God gave us a spirit not of fear but of power, love, and self-control." You are not growing alone. The Holy Spirit is your teacher, your encourager, your strength. When you feel weak, He empowers you. When you feel stuck, He pushes you forward. And when you are ready to give up, He reminds you who you are.

One of the enemy's greatest tactics is to convince you that you are not growing, that nothing is happening, that your prayers are hitting the ceiling, that your efforts are in vain. But do not be fooled by feelings. Growth often happens underground before it ever breaks the surface.

Just because it is not visible does not mean it is not valuable. God sees what is happening inside you, and He is not disappointed. He is invested.

Teaching Spotlight – Week 6: Developmental Potential

Before there is promotion, there is process. Before there is platform, there is pruning. God never sends an unprepared vessel to carry the weight of divine purpose. He develops in the dark what He intends to display in the light.

It is in the hidden places, the waiting rooms, the dry spells, the wilderness seasons, where character is forged and clarity is formed. Development does not always feel like destiny. It can feel like delay. But delay is not denial. It is often design. **Job 23:10** says, "But He knoweth the way that I take: when He hath tried me, I shall come forth

as gold." Gold is not discovered polished; it is purified through fire.

God is not in a rush to get you "there," He is committed to making sure you are ready when you arrive. That means letting some things die so something deeper can live. Letting ego be crucified so humility can rise. Letting immaturity be stripped so fruitfulness can emerge. These are not punishments. They are prophetic preparations.

Developmental potential is Heaven's training ground. It is where God stretches your capacity and deepens your dependency. You are not just learning how to carry the weight, you are learning how to carry it without losing your worship. You are learning how to move with grace, respond with wisdom, and speak with authority that has been earned through obedience.

Many people want the crown but resist the cross. They want influence without formation. But God's process does not bypass the soul, it sanctifies it. What He is building in you now may not be seen by others, but it is known by Heaven. And when the time comes, what was forged in secret will have the strength to stand in public.

Do not despise this season. This is not punishment, this is precision. This is where you are learning to lead from a deeper place. This is where He trusts you enough to train you. Let Him finish the work. Because what is being developed now is the version of you that will carry revival, not for a moment, but for a movement.

Kingdom Journal Week 6 Developmental Potential

WHEN POTENTIAL MEETS PURPOSE

Week 7 – Situational Potential

Maybe you have asked God, "Why am I here?" You thought by now you would be further along. More recognized. More fulfilled. But every door seems closed, and every effort feels unseen.

Let me remind you, the silence does not mean you have been forgotten. It may mean you are being formed.

God does not rush greatness. He allows tension to build resilience. He allows detours to birth discernment. And sometimes, He allows disappointment to redirect your destiny. Not as punishment, but as preparation.

You might be serving in a job that feels too small for your calling. You might be caregiving, grieving, waiting, rebuilding. Whatever it is, know this: this moment is not meaningless.

Ask the Holy Spirit to open your eyes to the divine activity around you. Who is watching your faithfulness? Who is being impacted by your consistency? What is God refining in your heart that comfort could never touch?

You do not have to wait for the next season to walk in purpose. Start now. Water the ground you are standing on. Encourage the people in front of you. Plant seeds, even when you feel overlooked.

God often promotes those who serve faithfully in obscurity. Do not try to escape the season, extract its wisdom.

Because when God finally opens the door, you will not just be ready, you will be refined.

Weekly Prayer

Father, thank You for using every situation in my life for Your glory. Teach me to see challenges as opportunities and obstacles as training grounds. When life feels uncertain, remind me that You are still in control. Help me to respond with faith instead of fear and to trust that You are working behind the scenes for my good. Use every circumstance, whether joyful or painful, to develop my character, deepen my faith, and advance Your purpose through me. In Jesus Name, Amen.

Romans 8:28

"And we know that all things work together for good to them that love God, to them who are the called according to his purpose."

Real-Life Reflection

A man once lost his job unexpectedly and felt like his world had fallen apart. Instead of giving up, he began praying for direction. Within months, he started a small business that not only sustained his family but created opportunities for others. What looked like a setback was actually a divine setup. Situations are not random, they are refinements. God uses circumstances to reveal capacity, reorder priorities, and redirect your path toward destiny.

Day 1 – Purpose in Pressure

Devotional: Pressure does not destroy potential, it reveals it. The same way oil comes from crushed olives, purpose is pressed out through life's pressures. God allows certain situations not to harm you, but to harvest what's inside of you. You carry strength you have never seen until life demands it.

Declaration: Pressure produces power in me.

Prayer: Lord, help me to see pressure as a sign that You are preparing me for something greater. Let the weight of this moment work for my good.

Prompt: What current pressure might God be using to strengthen your faith or focus?

Action Step: Instead of complaining about the pressure, write a declaration of purpose that speaks to what God is producing through it.

Day 2 – Seeing God in Every Season

Devotional: God is present in every season, whether the mountain or the valley, the rain or the drought. When you cannot trace His hand, trust His heart. Situational potential means seeing His purpose even

when life feels unpredictable. Every season has a reason, and nothing is wasted in God's timing.

Declaration: I will look for God's purpose in every season of my life.

Prayer: Father, open my eyes to see You in all circumstances. Let me discern Your purpose even when life feels unclear.

Prompt: What season are you currently in, and where can you see evidence of God's hand at work?

Action Step: Reflect on one past season that once confused you but later made sense and thank God for His perfect timing.

Day 3 – Responding with Faith

Devotional: Your response determines your result. Situations may be unpredictable, but your reaction can still be intentional. Faith does not deny the reality of struggle; it declares the truth of victory. When you respond in faith, you activate Heaven's intervention.

Declaration: I choose faith over frustration.

Prayer: Lord, teach me to respond with faith when life surprises me. Help me to guard my heart and speak Your Word over every situation.

Prompt: How have your words or attitudes shaped past outcomes in difficult situations?

Action Step: Speak one faith-filled confession over a current challenge and declare God's promise daily this week.

Day 4 – Turning Setbacks into Setups

Devotional: What the enemy meant for evil, God will always turn for good. Joseph's life proved that divine purpose can rise out of painful situations. A setback in the natural can become a setup in the Spirit. Every closed door redirects you to the right one. Do not waste time asking, "why me?" ask "what now, Lord?"

Declaration: Every setback in my life is setting me up for greater purpose.

Prayer: Father, turn every disappointment into divine direction. Let me see how You are positioning me for progress.

Prompt: Think of a time when a disappointment later became a blessing in disguise. What did it teach you about God's plan?

Action Step: Reframe one current challenge by writing out how it could be preparing you for your next level.

Day 5 – Standing Strong in Uncertainty

Devotional: Faith does not remove uncertainty; it stabilizes you in the middle of it. Situations may shift, but God's Word remains the same. When you stand firm on His promises, circumstances lose their power to shake you. Stability in storms reveals maturity in faith.

Declaration: I will stand strong because God stands with me.

Prayer: Lord, when I feel unsure, remind me that You are unchanging. Strengthen my faith to stand firm on Your Word.

Prompt: Where in your life do you need to stand firm despite uncertainty?

Action Step: Write out three scriptures about God's faithfulness and speak them over your situation daily.

Week 7 Kingdom Expansion: Situational Potential

Teaching Spotlight: What the Bible Says

Throughout Scripture, God consistently uses situations, good and bad, to develop people for purpose.

Consider Joseph. Betrayed by his brothers, sold into slavery, falsely imprisoned. His situation screamed defeat. But in **Genesis 50:20,** he declares: "You intended to harm me, but God intended it for good to accomplish what is now being done…" What others meant for evil, God used for elevation.

Or David. After being anointed as king, he returned to the pasture, not the palace. God used the sheepfold to train his hands for battle. Long before David faced Goliath, he was fighting lions and bears in

secret.

And what about Jesus? He spent thirty years in obscurity before ever performing a miracle. If the Son of God could be hidden for a season, so can you.

Your situation may feel insignificant, but it is sacred in the hands of God. He uses the unseen to prepare you for the unforgettable.

Teaching Spotlight – Week 7: Situational Potential

Sometimes purpose shows up in unfamiliar places. Not every divine assignment begins with a dream or an open door. Sometimes, it begins with discomfort. Detours. Dead ends. But even in these, God is not silent, He is strategic.

Romans 8:28 reminds us, "And we know that all things work together for good to them that love God, to them who are the called according to his purpose." All things. Not just the holy moments. Not just the victories or answered prayers. But the heartbreaks, the delays, the layoffs, the transitions. God is masterful at weaving what seems broken into something beautiful.

Situational potential is the prophetic ability to recognize God's hand in the very place you wish you were not. It is realizing that the storm did not stop your purpose, it activated it. That even the pain you did not choose can become the soil for the breakthrough you did not expect. Think of Joseph, his dream did not die in the pit or the prison. It was being shaped there. Elevated there. Preserved there.

The enemy wants you to misinterpret your current season. He wants you to believe that because it is hard, it must not be holy. But some of the most pivotal moments in your destiny will arise from inconvenient situations. The job you did not plan to take. The city you did not plan to move to. The role you did not feel ready for. These are not mistakes, they are movement.

God will use unexpected places to unlock hidden dimensions of your calling. Where you are now may not look like prophecy, but it may be

the precise route to fulfillment. Do not abort the process just because it is uncomfortable. If God planted you here, there is something in this soil meant to grow you. There is oil in this assignment, even if it does not look like what you prayed for.

You do not have to understand it to be developed by it. You only need to remain faithful, discerning, and available. Trust that this situation is not in the way of your purpose, it is part of the way.

WHEN POTENTIAL MEETS PURPOSE

_____

_____

_____

_____

_____

_____

_____

_____

_____

_____

_____

_____

_____

_____

_____

_____

_____

_____

_____

_____

_____

_____

_____

WHEN POTENTIAL MEETS PURPOSE

Week 8 – Unlocking Potential

Maybe you have been sitting on a dream because you are afraid to fail. Maybe you have been shrinking in rooms you were called to lead in. Or maybe your past whispers so loudly that you have stopped believing you are worthy of more.

But here is the truth: the enemy is not afraid of your history; he is terrified of your unlocked future.

He knows that once you realize what you carry, once you embrace your God-given authority, you become a threat to every lie, every generational curse, and every stronghold.

So how do you unlock potential?

You start by renouncing every lie you have believed.
You forgive yourself for what happened.
You receive healing in the places you have been hiding.
You give God your yes, not just once, but daily.

And then, you move. You speak. You create. You mentor. You serve. You step forward, even when you feel scared. Because courage is not the absence of fear, it is obedience in the face of it.

You may not feel "ready." But you are already called.
You may not feel "qualified." But you are already chosen.

The key is not perfection; the key is truth. And once you unlock it, your potential begins to breathe. It begins to build. It begins to bless others.

You are not meant to live behind a locked door. You are the door God wants to open to others.

Weekly Prayer

Father, thank You for the treasures You have placed inside of me. Help me to recognize, stir, and release every gift You have given. Remove fear, doubt, and hesitation, and replace them with faith, courage, and clarity. Teach me to move when You say move and to trust that what You have deposited in me is enough for the assignment ahead. Let this be the season where my potential becomes power in action. In Jesus Name, Amen.

2 Timothy 1:6

"Wherefore I put thee in remembrance that thou stir up the gift of God, which is in thee by the putting on of my hands."

Real-Life Reflection

A young believer once prayed for God to send her opportunities to use her gifts. The answer did not come as a stage or spotlight; it came as a simple request to serve at her church's outreach. That small act of obedience revealed her passion for leadership, teaching, and compassion. Every opportunity you accept in faith is a key that unlocks something inside of you. Potential is not unlocked by waiting, it is released by doing.

Day 1 – Stirring the Gift Within

Devotional: Every believer carries divine deposits waiting to be stirred. Stirring requires movement, faith, prayer, and obedience. Dormant gifts awaken when you refuse to stay idle. You do not need a title to operate in your gift; you only need willingness.

Declaration: I will stir up the gift of God within me.

Prayer: Lord, show me what You have placed inside of me. Teach me how to activate and steward the gifts You have given.

Prompt: What spiritual or natural gift has been lying dormant that God may be calling you to stir again?

Action Step: Write one practical way you can begin using that gift this week.

Day 2 – The Power of Belief

Devotional: You cannot unlock what you do not believe you have. Faith is the master key that releases potential. When you believe what God says about you, heaven backs your actions with power. Unbelief locks doors that were meant to open.

Declaration: I believe God's Word about who I am and what I can do.

WHEN POTENTIAL MEETS PURPOSE

Prayer: Father, strengthen my faith to believe that You have equipped me for every good work.

Prompt: What belief about yourself needs to shift for you to fully embrace your potential?

Action Step: Write a new faith statement that aligns with what God says about you and speak it daily.

Day 3 – Faith in Action

Devotional: Faith without works is dormant potential. You unlock what is inside of you by moving forward, even in uncertainty. The miracle is rarely in the plan; it is in the step. When you act in obedience, you give God permission to multiply your effort.

Declaration: My faith unlocks doors that fear tried to close.

Prayer: Lord, help me to act on what I know instead of waiting until I understand it all. Give me courage to move in faith.

Prompt: What step of faith have you been delaying that could activate a new level of growth?

Action Step: Take one concrete action this week that demonstrates faith in motion.

Day 4 – Doors of Opportunity

Devotional: Every act of obedience opens a new door. God places opportunities along your path to test readiness and reveal responsibility. Some doors will not open until you knock; others will not appear until you start walking. When you stay faithful in small things, greater doors unfold naturally.

Declaration: God is opening doors that align with my divine purpose.

Prayer: Father, prepare me for every door You are opening. Give me wisdom to walk through what is from You and discernment to avoid distractions.

Prompt: What door of opportunity might God be inviting you to walk through right now?

WHEN POTENTIAL MEETS PURPOSE

Action Step: Identify one open door and prayerfully commit to stepping through it this week.

Day 5 – Walking in Fullness

Devotional: Unlocking potential leads to walking in fullness, the place where purpose and power unite. Fullness is not about perfection; it is about continual surrender and obedience. As you walk in what God has revealed, He will unveil even more. The journey of potential never ends; it expands.

Declaration: I walk in the fullness of who God created me to be.

Prayer: Lord, thank You for calling me into fullness. Help me to remain humble, faithful, and fruitful as I walk out my purpose.

Prompt: What does "walking in fullness" look like in your current season?

Action Step: Write one personal declaration that captures how you intend to live out your unlocked potential daily.

Week 8 Kingdom Expansion: Unlocking Potential

Teaching Spotlight: What the Bible Says

Proverbs 23:7 says, "As a man thinks in his heart, so is he." What you believe about yourself shapes how you show up in the world. If you believe you are unworthy, you will shrink back from opportunity. If you believe you are broken beyond repair, you will never pursue wholeness.

But when you believe what God says about you, that you are chosen (Ephesians 1:4), empowered (2 Peter 1:3), and filled with divine purpose, you begin to walk differently. You speak with more boldness. You make decisions with more faith.

Galatians 2:20 reminds us: "It is no longer I who live, but Christ lives in me…"

This means you do not have to rely on your strength to

unlock your future. The Spirit of God inside you hold the keys. He reveals, convicts, heals, and emboldens you. You are not stuck; you are being stirred.

> *You were not created to live in spiritual captivity. You were born to walk in freedom, unchained, unashamed, and fully alive in purpose.*

Teaching Spotlight – Week 8: Unlocking Potential

Potential does not die; it gets buried. Buried under fear, failure, trauma, or years of rejection. But buried is not the same as gone. And when God speaks, what was dormant begins to rise.

Isaiah 1:19 declares, "If ye be willing and obedient, ye shall eat the good of the land." Willingness and obedience are the keys that unlock what has been trapped inside. God is not waiting for your perfection; He is waiting for your permission. He does not ask you to be flawless; He asks you to be available.

Unlocking potential starts with surrender. It begins when you decide that the mask must come off, that the wounds must be healed, and that the false identities must be laid down. As long as you are pretending, you are protecting the very shell God is trying to break. But when truth and transparency collide with grace, resurrection happens.

This is the chapter where shame loses its grip and silence breaks. Where what you thought disqualified, you become the very thing God uses to deliver others. What felt like a limitation was actually a lock, and now the key is in your hand. Every time you tell your story, you turn it. Every time you forgive, you rotate it. Every time you take a step toward healing, you hear the sound of the unlocking.

But remember, potential does not unlock automatically. It responds to obedience. It reacts to hunger. It activates through intimacy with the Father. The more you walk with Him, the more you see what He

has placed in you. And what once felt unreachable suddenly becomes recognizable.

You do not need another prophetic word; you need the courage to act on the last one. The prison doors are open. The chains are loose. But you still have to rise. You still have to walk out. You still have to believe that who God says you are more real than what you have been through.

Unlocking potential means you stop shrinking to fit who you were and start expanding into who you are becoming. It means you say yes, not because you are ready, but because you are His.

WHEN POTENTIAL MEETS PURPOSE

_____

_____

_____

_____

_____

_____

_____

_____

_____

_____

_____

_____

_____

_____

_____

_____

_____

_____

_____

_____

_____

WHEN POTENTIAL MEETS PURPOSE

Week 9 – Maximizing Potential

You have come a long way. You have identified your gifts. You have recognized your calling. But now comes the hard, holy work: turning your "yes" into a lifestyle.

Maximizing potential means showing up even when no one claps. It means practicing excellence in private. It means choosing discipline over distraction, again and again.

Maybe you have been delaying obedience, waiting for a better time, clearer instructions, or more confidence. But what if God is saying, "I'm waiting for you to move with what you already have"?

Your next level does not require perfection, it requires stewardship.

Take the class. Launch the ministry. Finish the manuscript. Mentor the teen. Serve faithfully. Rest strategically. Create margin. Build systems. Sharpen your skills. You do not need a bigger stage; you need a bolder yes.

Because someone's freedom is connected to your obedience.

And when it gets hard, when momentum slows and motivation fades, remind yourself: God gave me this for a reason. My diligence is worship. My follow-through is legacy.

You were not created to bury your gift. You were made to multiply it.

Weekly Prayer

Father, thank You for every gift, resource, and opportunity You have entrusted to me. Teach me to be a faithful steward of what I have right now. Deliver me from procrastination, fear, and comparison, and help me to focus on the assignment in front of me. Strengthen my consistency and sharpen my discipline so that I can multiply what You have placed in my hands. I do not want to just start well; I want to finish strong. Use my diligence to bring You glory. In Jesus Name, Amen.

Luke 16:10

"He that is faithful in that which is least is faithful also in much: and he that is unjust in the least is unjust also in much."

Real-Life Reflection

A man once prayed for greater opportunities in ministry but overlooked the ones already before him. When he decided to give his best to the small Bible study he led, God began to multiply his reach. His consistency in the small prepared him for the greater. Potential grows through stewardship. God rewards not size, but faithfulness. When you maximize what is in your hand, He releases what is in your heart.

Day 1 – The Discipline of Potential

Devotional: Potential without discipline becomes wasted possibility. Discipline keeps you aligned when emotion fades. The most gifted people are not always the most successful, those who are consistent are. God blesses order and diligence. Every moment you choose discipline; you are building a foundation for destiny.

Declaration: I am disciplined and diligent with what God has placed in my hands.

Prayer: Lord, help me to develop the habits that protect my purpose. Strengthen my focus and remove distractions that limit my growth.

Prompt: What area of your life requires more discipline to fully reach your potential?

Action Step: Identify one daily routine or habit you can strengthen this week to stay focused on your purpose.

Day 2 – Stewarding What You have Been Given

Devotional: God never gives increase where there is neglect. Stewardship means managing well what you already have. Before God multiplies, He measures faithfulness. Whether it is time, talent, or

treasure, how you handle it determines your next level. Excellence is not perfection; it is intentional care for what God has entrusted.

Declaration: I am a faithful steward of every gift and opportunity.

Prayer: Father, teach me to value what I have been given and to use it for Your glory. Let my stewardship prepare me for greater responsibility.

Prompt: What have you been given that you could handle with greater excellence or attention?

Action Step: Make a small but intentional improvement in how you manage your current responsibilities.

Day 3 – Consistency Creates Capacity

Devotional: Consistency increases capacity. Every act of faith, prayer, and obedience expands your ability to handle more. God builds capacity through consistency, not comfort. The more consistent you are, the stronger your spiritual muscle becomes. Growth happens when you keep showing up.

Declaration: My consistency is creating capacity for greater impact.

Prayer: Lord, help me to remain steadfast in my commitments. Even when progress feels slow, remind me that faithfulness is never wasted.

Prompt: In what area do you need to be more consistent to see long-term results?

Action Step: Set one clear goal this week that requires daily consistency and track your progress.

WHEN POTENTIAL MEETS PURPOSE

Day 4 – Excellence in the Everyday

Devotional: Excellence is worship expressed through work. It is not about perfection; it is about doing your best as unto the Lord. When you give your best in ordinary moments, God turns them into extraordinary outcomes. Excellence in the everyday sets you apart and positions you for elevation.

Declaration: I pursue excellence as an act of worship to God.

Prayer: Father, let my work reflect Your excellence. Help me to honor You in every detail of my daily life.

Prompt: How can you demonstrate excellence in your ordinary routine this week?

Action Step: Choose one daily task to elevate by adding intentionality, joy, or prayer to it.

Day 5 – Finishing Strong

Devotional: Starting is easy, finishing requires endurance. God is not looking for perfection, but perseverance. You finish strong when you stay faithful to your "yes." Every assignment completed in obedience brings Him glory. Your ability to finish well is proof that potential has matured into purpose.

Declaration: I will finish strong and fulfill my divine assignment.

Prayer: Lord, give me endurance to finish what I started. Strengthen my decision making and renew my vision so I do not grow weary in doing good.

Prompt: What area of your life do you need renewed strength to finish well?

Action Step: Write one unfinished task or goal that you will commit to complete this week with God's help.

WHEN POTENTIAL MEETS PURPOSE

Week 9 Kingdom Expansion: Maximizing Potential

Teaching Spotlight: What the Bible Says

In **Matthew 25,** Jesus tells the Parable of the Talents. One servant receives five talents and multiplies it. Another receives two and does the same. But the third, fearful and hesitant, hides his one talent in the ground.

The master's response is sobering. To the fruitful servants, he says, "Well done, good and faithful servant." But to the one who buried his gift, he says, "You wicked, lazy servant."

Let that sink in. Inaction is not neutral, its rebellion wrapped in fear.

God is not looking for flash; He is looking for faithfulness. And faithfulness is measured in how you steward what you have been given, whether five talents or one.

Philippians 3:12 echoes this pursuit: "Not that I have already obtained all this… but I press on to take hold of that for which Christ Jesus took hold of me."

That is what maximizing potential looks like. A holy pursuit. A pressing forward. Not because we are trying to earn God's love, but because we are determined to honor it.

The enemy of fruitfulness is not failure, it is comfort. Comfort convinces you that "almost" is enough. But you were not called to almost build, almost believe. You were called to finish strong.

Teaching Spotlight – Week 9: Maximizing Potential

Potential is the raw material of purpose, but it is not the final product. It must be shaped, stretched, and stewarded. God never anoints you just to impress others, He anoints you to build, multiply, and impact nations. This is not the season to sit on what you carry. This is the hour to pour it out.

WHEN POTENTIAL MEETS PURPOSE

Luke 12:48 declares, "To whom much is given, much shall be required." That is not a warning, it is an invitation. You have been trusted with something sacred. Heaven has deposited vision, gifting, and divine ideas into you. But potential alone is not what produces Kingdom fruit, obedience, discipline, and focus do.

Maximizing potential requires movement. It is not about being busy, it is about being intentional. Every hour you dedicate to refining your skill, every late night you spend in study or prayer, every time you invest in development instead of distraction, you are declaring: "Lord, I will not bury what You gave me."

This is not hustle culture. This is holy urgency. Your diligence is worship. Your structure is stewardship. The servant in Matthew 25 who multiplied his talents did not have more gifting, he had more commitment. He had vision for the return. The one who buried his gift was called wicked, not because he lacked ability, but because he lacked action.

Let this truth sink into your spirit: God expects a return on what He has placed in you, not because He is demanding, but because He knows the value of what He deposited. You have already seen glimpses of your calling. You have already felt the nudge to create, to write, to build, to lead. Now comes the invitation to develop what you have discovered.

You will not drift into destiny. You must decide to become. It is not enough to recognize potential; you must maximize it. That means saying no to comfort. It means showing up when no one is clapping. It means sharpening your edge and stretching your capacity. Not someday, today.

The world is waiting on what is inside of you. But Heaven is waiting on your yes.

WHEN POTENTIAL MEETS PURPOSE

WHEN POTENTIAL MEETS PURPOSE

Week 10 – When Potential Meets Purpose

Take a moment. Breathe it in. This is what purpose feels like. It is not always loud. Sometimes it is the quiet confidence that your life matters. That your obedience is holy. That your yes carries weight in Heaven.
You may have once doubted your worth. Hid behind comparison. Questioned your gifts. But look at you now. Growing. Healing. Rising. Saying yes even when it is hard. Living with intention even when it is uncomfortable.

That is purpose. It is not always about doing more, it is about becoming more of who God created you to be.

You do not need to wait for another confirmation. You have been prepared. You have been refined. Now it is time to walk it out, not in striving, but in surrender.

Lead with love. Build with boldness. Serve with joy. Speak with truth. Heal with compassion. Create with courage. Rest with assurance.

And when doubt comes, because it will, remind yourself: "I am not here by accident. I am walking in what God prepared for me."

This is your season. This is your assignment. This is the collision you have been praying for.

Live it loud. Live it free. Live it on purpose.

Weekly Prayer

Father, thank You for every season that has shaped me, every lesson that has refined me, and every promise that has carried me. Today, I surrender fully to Your plan. Let everything You have placed within me align with Your divine timing. I am no longer waiting for purpose to find me; I am walking in it. Use my life as a vessel of Your glory. Let my potential collide with destiny so that others may see You through me. In Jesus Name, Amen.

Scripture Meditation

Jeremiah 1:5

"Before I formed thee in the belly I knew thee; and before thou camest

WHEN POTENTIAL MEETS PURPOSE

forth out of the womb I sanctified thee, and I ordained thee a prophet unto the nations."

Romans 8:30

"Moreover, whom he did predestinate, them he also called: and whom he called, them he also justified: and whom he justified, them he also glorified."

Real-Life Reflection

A young woman once struggled to understand her calling. She served faithfully, worked quietly, and wondered if her life truly mattered. One day, God reminded her that purpose is not proven by platform, it is revealed by obedience. She realized that her potential had always been pointing toward something greater: purpose in action. When potential meets purpose, you no longer strive, you flow. Every experience, mistake, and miracle becomes a thread in God's masterpiece.

Day 1 – The Moment of Alignment

Devotional: When potential meets purpose, alignment happens. Everything you have learned, endured, and prayed through begins to make sense. God does not waste seasons; He weaves them together for destiny. Alignment is when what is in you finally agrees with what God has always spoken about you.

Declaration: I am aligned with the will and timing of God.

Prayer: Lord, align my heart, mind, and actions with Your purpose. Let every gift and lesson find its rightful place in Your plan.

Prompt: What moment in your life do you believe God used to align you closer to your calling?

Action Step: Write a brief reflection on how your past experiences have prepared you for your current purpose.

Day 2 – Purpose Revealed Through Obedience

Devotional: Purpose is rarely revealed in comfort. It unfolds through obedience. Each "yes" to God unlocks another layer of destiny. When you obey in small things, you activate divine momentum in great things. Purpose is not something you chase, it is something you walk into by faith.

Declaration: My obedience opens the door to my destiny.

Prayer: Father, give me the courage to obey even when the outcome is unclear. Help me to trust that my obedience is the bridge to purpose.

Prompt: What is one area where God is calling you to obey immediately?

Action Step: Take one step of obedience today, even if it feels small. Watch how peace follows obedience.

Day 3 – Living Beyond Limitations

Devotional: When purpose takes root, limitations lose power. What once intimidated you now inspires you. God uses purpose to reveal strength you did not know you had. Stop rehearsing what you cannot do and start remembering who called you. The same God who gave you potential is the One who empowers your purpose.

Declaration: I am not limited by fear, doubt, or past mistakes.

Prayer: Lord, break every limitation I have believed about myself. Expand my vision and renew my confidence in Your ability within me.

Prompt: What limitation have you believed that God is now challenging you to overcome?

Action Step: Replace one limiting thought with a declaration of faith and repeat it daily this week.

Day 4 – The Fulfillment of Promise

Devotional: Every promise God made is attached to purpose. Fulfillment does not come through striving, but through surrender. When you allow Him to finish what He started, your life becomes living proof that God keeps His Word. Purpose is promise in motion, it is heaven's "yes" manifesting on earth.

Declaration: God is fulfilling His promises in my life right now.

Prayer: Father, thank You for being faithful to complete what You began. I trust Your timing and receive every promise that aligns with Your will.

Prompt: What promise from God are you currently waiting on, and how can you remain faithful while you wait?

Action Step: Write a prayer of thanksgiving for one promise that God has already fulfilled in your life.

Day 5 – The Kingdom in Motion

Devotional: When potential meets purpose, the Kingdom advances. You are not just gifted, you are commissioned. Every skill, every word, every act of service becomes Kingdom currency. Walking in purpose means living intentionally, knowing that your life is part of something eternal. Purpose transforms influence into impact.

Declaration: I am a vessel of purpose, moving in Kingdom power.

Prayer: Lord, let my life bring Your Kingdom to earth. Use my voice, my hands, and my heart to reveal Your glory to others.

Prompt: How can your daily life reflect the Kingdom of God more intentionally?

Action Step: Do one purposeful act this week that demonstrates God's love and power to someone else.

WHEN POTENTIAL MEETS PURPOSE

Week 10 Kingdom Expansion: When Potential Meets Purpose

Teaching Spotlight: What the Bible Says

Jeremiah 1:5 says, "Before I formed you in the womb I knew you, before you were born, I set you apart…"
This means your purpose did not begin when you figured it out. It began before your first breath. Heaven assigned you long before earth acknowledged you.

First Corinthians 10:31 reminds us, "Whatever you do, do it all for the glory of God." That includes conversations, caregiving, leadership, parenting, business, and creativity. Purpose is not limited to platforms; it flourishes in obedience.

Purpose is not about spotlight; it is about assignment.

And when your potential collides with that assignment, things shift. You no longer need permission. You walk in authority. You no longer perform for affirmation. You move from conviction. You no longer ask, "Why me?" Instead, you declare, "Send me."

When potential meets purpose, you do not just live life, you release destiny.

Teaching Spotlight – Week 10: When Potential Meets Purpose

There is a divine moment, one marked not by applause, but by alignment, when everything you have carried, suffered, endured, and overcome begins to make sense. This is that moment. The wilderness taught you worship. The delay refined your discernment. The pain gave you oil. Now the promise is calling.

Isaiah 30:21 declares, "And thine ears shall hear a word behind thee, saying, This is the way, walk ye in it…" You are no longer waiting for clarity. You are walking in it. This is not the season to keep questioning what God has already confirmed. This is the time to move with

confidence because what you once called potential; Heaven is now calling purpose.

Purpose is not a place. It is a posture. It is not a title. It is a testimony. Purpose is what happens when your obedience catches up to your anointing, when your internal yes collides with Heaven's timing. It is not about perfection; it is about surrender. And when potential and purpose finally meet, your life becomes a living epistle, read by generations and remembered by eternity.

Every trial you have walked through was training. Every silent prayer was planting. You did not just survive; you were being sculpted. And now, the version of you that emerges is not afraid, unsure, or unworthy. You are appointed. You are released. You are ready.

This is not about performance. This is about fulfillment. You are not just carrying the dream anymore; you are the dream in motion. This is the place where your preparation becomes prophecy fulfilled. This is where your voice shakes atmospheres. Where your yes shakes nations. Where your scars shine with the oil of surrender.

When potential meets purpose, impact becomes inevitable. You stop striving and start flowing. You stop hiding and start declaring. You stop rehearsing rejection and start releasing revelation. Because you have not only found your lane, you have been lit with fire to run it.

You were never meant to live full. You were born to empty yourself into your assignment, to pour out all Heaven put in, and to hear the words: "Well done."

_____

_____

_____

_____

_____

_____

_____

_____

_____

_____

_____

_____

_____

_____

_____

_____

_____

_____

_____

_____

_____

FINAL CHARGE

You were born for more.

This is not the end of a chapter ; it is the beginning of
a movement. The stirring inside of you is not random.
It is divine evidence that Heaven has assigned you to
manifest potential and walk boldly in purpose.

Every seed of identity that was reclaimed...
Every fear that was confronted...
Every step of growth, surrender, and obedience...

It has brought you to a tipping point ; where your power
must be activated, your voice must be heard, your presence
must be felt, and your purpose must be lived.

No more shrinking. No more delay. No more questioning whether
you are enough. You are not behind; you are right on time. You
carry weight in the spirit. You are a carrier of glory. You were called
to be a Kingdom solution in the earth. The world is not waiting
for another copy. It is waiting for your authentic obedience.

So rise.
Build.
Speak.
Serve.
Move.
Become.

Let every page of this book become fuel in your belly and fire
in your bones. Let your "yes" echo through every assignment,
every room, every generation. May the heavens respond to your
obedience and the earth reap the fruit of your surrender.

You are where power meets purpose. You are
the answer someone is praying for.

Now go. Unlock. Activate. Advance. Because destiny is waiting.

PROPHETIC INVITATION INTO GOD'S KINGDOM

ROMANS 10:8–11

But what saith it? The word is nigh thee, even in thy mouth, and in thy heart: that is, the word of faith, which we preach; That if thou shalt confess with thy mouth the Lord Jesus, and shalt believe in thine heart that God hath raised him from the dead, thou shalt be saved.

For with the heart man believeth unto righteousness; and with the mouth confession is made unto salvation. For the scripture saith, Whosoever believeth on him shall not be ashamed.

Come.

This is your divine moment of invitation. Heaven is not far, it is near. The Word is already in your mouth and written upon your heart. This is not a distant call. It is immediate, personal, and holy. God is not asking for perfection; He is drawing you with love.

You are not just being saved from something; you are being called into something, into a Kingdom that cannot be shaken. A Kingdom where identity is restored, voice carries authority, and life becomes a divine assignment. This is not religion; this is relationship. This is redemption.

Let every excuse fall. Let every delay be broken. Let every lie lose its grip. The voice of God is near. The Kingdom is at hand. His Spirit is reaching for you now.

You were never meant to live at the mercy of the world's systems. You were born for dominion. To carry light in dark places. To reveal Jesus in your generation. To walk in righteousness, not religion.

The altar is not a stage, it is your heart. And the confession is not complicated. Believe. Speak. Receive. Rise.

Say yes to the King. Say yes to purpose. Say yes to the divine

WHEN POTENTIAL MEETS PURPOSE

exchange, where your ashes become beauty, your shame becomes strength, and your voice becomes a trumpet for Heaven's call.

This is more than salvation, it is your sending. You are not just entering the Kingdom. You are becoming an ambassador of it.

So step forward. Speak what God says. Believe what He promised. Walk in what He has prepared. The Kingdom is calling. Say yes.

WHEN POTENTIAL MEETS PURPOSE

ABOUT THE AUTHORS

Ambassador Melissa McDuffie answered the call to ministry in 2001 under the leadership of Pastor James A. Owens at Lincolnville Baptist Church. Upon accepting the divine call God placed on her life, she began to faithfully preach and teach the Gospel of Jesus Christ. Melissa lives by Romans 10:9, which declares, "If you confess with your mouth and believe in your heart that Jesus is Lord, you will be saved." She is a visionary leader, mentor, and servant of God with a heart for empowering people to rise beyond limitations. Her work in ministry and the community has transformed lives through identity coaching, spiritual development, and purpose, driven leadership. She brings wisdom, compassion, and insight to everything she does, especially in helping others see what God sees in them.

Ambassador Kenneth McDuffie answered the call to ministry in 2011 under the leadership of Pastor Jerry and Agnes Green at Perfecting the Heart Worship Center. Upon accepting the divine call God placed on his life, he began to faithfully preach and teach the Gospel of Jesus Christ. Kenneth lives by Romans 10:9, which declares, "If you confess with your mouth and believe in your heart that Jesus is Lord, you will be saved." He is a dedicated Kingdom Ambassador, minister, teacher, and motivator. His passion lies in equipping others with biblical truth, prophetic clarity, and practical tools for victorious living. With years of experience in ministry leadership and mentoring, Kenneth is committed to Unlocking divine within every believer.

Their unwavering commitment to God led to elevation and greater responsibility, serving under Pastor Jerry Greene of Perfecting the Heart Worship Center in Chester, South Carolina. There, Melissa and Kenneth served as an Evangelists and as members of the Board of Directors. It was during this time that they met and later married. Together, the McDuffies embarked on a deeper season of spiritual training under the leadership of Apostle Raquel D. Broadie, Overseer of the Restoration Apostolic International Network in Charlotte, NC. After much prayer and seeking the Lord, they obeyed God's call to shepherd His people in Chester, South Carolina, where they founded Repairer of the Breach Evangelistic Ministry.

Today, the McDuffies continue to serve faithfully in ministry as

WHEN POTENTIAL MEETS PURPOSE

Apostles under the spiritual covering of Apostle DC Sr. and Apostle Tara Terry of The Kingdom Learning Center. They are committed to equipping believers, perfecting the saints, and edifying the Body of Christ for Kingdom advancement. They also carry out a prison ministry in Chester County, preaching freedom to those who are physically bound yet called to live free in spirit.

Their ministry operates under the authority of the Holy Spirit, with signs, wonders, and miracles following.